Desktop

F I R E

EXTINGUISHER

T0364042

Copyright © 2020 by Running Press
Illustrations copyright © 2020 by Adam Howling

Hachette Book Group supports the right to free
expression and the value of copyright. The purpose
of copyright is to encourage writers and artists to
produce the creative works that enrich our culture.

The scanning, uploading, and distribution of this
book without permission is a theft of the author's
intellectual property. If you would like permission to
use material from the book (other than for review
purposes), please contact permissions@hbgusa.com.
Thank you for your support of the author's rights.

RP Minis®
Hachette Book Group
1290 Avenue of the Americas, New York, NY 10104
www.runningpress.com
@Running_Press

Published by RP Minis, an imprint of Perseus Books,
LLC, a subsidiary of Hachette Book Group, Inc. The
RP Minis name and logo is a registered trademark
of the Hachette Book Group.

ISBN: 978-0-7624-7373-1

CONTENTS

Have an Office Fire? Don't Stress— Put It Out!

PUT OUT A FIRE
[PŬT OUT UH FAHYUHR]

(idiomatic) To handle a problem, especially a sudden and unexpected one, caused by the negligence, ineptitude, or misbehavior of another person.

There are many perils to our always-on, notification-driven, everything-is-urgent modern world. There's a crisis! This is an emergency! Time is critical! Sometimes it seems like the second you switch your computer on, or stroll into work with your foamy latte, everything is on fire. And, of course, it always falls to you to put it out.

Turns out your new admin deleted that really important file that your boss needed for a meeting today. The bank called and your deposits didn't go through, and payroll is tomorrow. Somehow, your vendor just shipped 10,000 of the wrong item, despite you confirming the order twice. And your flippant colleague just mistook the new client for an intern and asked them to fetch some coffee. On top of all of that, you have to be careful that all of the glowing embers from yesterday's fires don't flare up again. How are you supposed to function with that kind of stress in your life?

Luckily for you, there's a solution for handling your office fires that doesn't involve you losing your mind: the Desktop Fire Extinguisher! Just aim at the blaze, press down the nozzle, and relax as the soothing *whoosh* sound—the sound of all your problems disappearing—vaporizes the tension.

Work gets messy and stressy. Keep your Desktop Fire Extinguisher close at hand for when life at the office boils over.

A Brief History of the Fire Extinguisher

The earliest "fire extinguishers" were people just carrying buckets of water from a well or a lake and passing them along a human chain. (I mean, imagine having to rely on *all* of your co-workers to help you extinguish the flames. Would your workplace simply become a pile of ash?)

Then, in the Middle Ages, "squirts" began to be used. They were sort of like the water pumps kids dip into a swimming pool these days—pulling up a plunger and pushing it back out again to squirt a tiny little jet of water at a fire. They actually used squirts later on during the 1666 Great Fire of London, which is perhaps why it turned out to be a

"great" fire as opposed to a fizzing out earlier.

Leonardo da Vinci actually developed the first sprinkler system (of course it's always him inventing something, isn't it?). It was involved in a hilarious dinner party gaffe in which he tried to create an automated system—kind of like a sushi conveyor belt—to bring food out from a kitchen for guests of the Duke of Milan. It misfired and the oven started burning the food; thus, the rudimentary sprinkler system he created triggered and soaked all of the food. The party was ruined, but on the plus side the sprinkler was really successful.

The first true fire extinguisher officially on record was patented by chemist Ambrose Godfrey in England in 1723. It was basically a cask of fire-extinguishing liquid with a chamber of gunpowder in the middle. The gunpowder was connected to a series of fuses which, when ignited, exploded the gunpowder and scattered the solution—the intention was that it scattered in the direction of the blaze, though it was a crapshoot. It wasn't the world's safest or most accurate apparatus, but the idea had legs. Later, in the early 1800s, Captain George William Manby patented the *Extincteur*, a portable cylinder of water that used compressed air to shoot it out of a narrow tube—the earliest iteration of the little fire extinguisher you hold in your hands today.

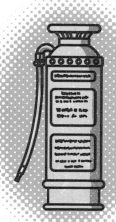

Newer generations of fire extinguishers haven't changed that much in design, save for the innards evolving to tackle different firefighting challenges—liquid fires, gas fires, electrical fires, grease fires, stunt-double fires, and smoldering metals all have their own approved fire extinguishers.

And now, you have *your* very own approved fire extinguisher, for all your incendiary office needs.

How to Use Your Desktop Fire Extinguisher

Your Desktop Fire Extinguisher is an invaluable asset to have close at hand, in case some of the reports you have piling up or a heap of customer service complaint memos somehow create the tinder for one of your workplace's big bonfires. Keep it next to your stapler or in an easy-to-reach filing cabinet for any number of heated happenings, such as the smoldery scenarios on the following pages.

SMOLDERY SCENARIO #1

Your customer service reps called out sick today (from partying too hard the night before), and this morning, your website broke.

Ah, yes, the downside of employee bonding, when they spend that time imbibing to excess and unable to function the next day. To top it off, the switchboard is lighting up with calls from folks who can't place an order, because today just happens to be the day your website decided to quit.

PUT IT OUT!

WHOOOOOOSH*

Press that nozzle and feel the rush of relaxation as the extinguisher snuffs out the sparks. Time to recruit the most lovely folks in your office to staff up the phone lines! After some time on the line with Joan from HR, your angry customers are assuaged—while you spend your time overseeing your IT team to get your business back online.

While on a video conference call with your client, your boss left themselves off mute while bad-mouthing the client under their breath.

Trusting that you've tamed the technology enough can really backfire. Your boss doesn't realize their mistake until it's too late— right about the time that your client irately inquires as to what the hell just happened.

PUT IT OUT!
WHOOOOOOOSH

Press that nozzle and delight in
the wave of relief that comes over
you as the extinguisher douses
the conflagration. After delicately
admonishing your boss via text
message, you immediately apologize
and whip up an excuse about the
stress your boss has been under
lately—and then quickly change the
subject to offer the client 50% off.

This morning at breakfast, your kid spilled an entire carafe of coffee all over the requested stack of investor presentation decks you spent all night printing out—and the presentation is in one hour.

You know, you'd think that such destruction couldn't possibly come from such a tiny human, but every chance your child gets they prove you wrong. You're left staring at a dripping pile of papery pulp, far from the recognizable and

orderly assemblage it was mere
seconds ago.

PUT IT OUT!
WHOOOOOOSH

Press that nozzle and enjoy the
reprieve as the extinguisher quenches
the inferno. Kindly guide your lovely
offspring back to the playpen.
Then thank your lucky stars that
you live in the online age, as you
simultaneously 1) assuage the entire

group of investors that they will be receiving beautifully bound copies of the presentation following your meeting and 2) place a rush order at Kinko's.

Your gem of an intern started an actual, literal office fire while trying to microwave leftovers in aluminum foil.

There are lots of things for young people to learn when they first enter the working world, though we already assume they have the basic knowledge to not zap a metal wrapper. But so it goes.

PUT IT OUT!
WHOOOOOOOSH

Press that nozzle and let out a big
sigh of relief as the extinguisher
cools the coals. Keep the microwave
door closed, unplug it, and send your
intern to both get a latte from the
coffee shop and a book about how
radiation works from the library.

After giving a big speech about how personalization is the key to success, and how it's incredibly important to pay attention to detail, your Board Chair receives an email addressed to "Dear _____, " .

It's not only the fact that the unfortunate oversight of a "Dear Blank" email happened to go straight to the Board Chair who made this very speech, it's exacerbated by the fact that it was sent to him only a half an hour after said speech. Now a whole phone chain of angry complaints has been activated. Yeesh.

PUT IT OUT!
WHOOOOOOOSH

Press that nozzle and pursue the palliative as the extinguisher sprays the hot spot. Assure your Board Chair that, of course, this won't happen again. Explain the idiosyncrasies of digital marketing until his head hurts a little bit, and subsequently produce a shiny report in which a revenue increase was correlated with an email. Then hire a proofreader.

SMOLDERY SCENARIO #6

When trying to promote your new pet cleaning product, the Slick Rag, your social media manager posts a tweet that says, "#SlickRag is the best thing to happen to animals in long time," not knowing that the hashtag #SlickRag is currently being used to comment on the Ragweed Wetlands Oil Spill.

Could there possibly be any *worse* timing in the world? You just encouraged your social media team to use more hashtags to

reach more potential customers,
and now you've announced to the
world that crude-covered wildlife is
your company's idea of a good time.

PUT IT OUT!
WHOOOOOOSH

Press that nozzle and alleviate your
agony as the extinguisher soaks
the blaze. Post a transparent and
earnest apology immediately, and
call up your accountant to make

a hearty donation to the clean-up fund. Can't hurt to encourage your social media team to search for a hashtag before using one, too.

In Case of
Emergency

You've never been more equipped to handle those fire-alarm fires that light up your cubicle on the daily. No more band-aid solutions or playing whack-a-mole. Breathe easy— you've got the only equipment you need to both lower your blood pressure and climb the corporate ladder. Pack your Desktop Fire Extinguisher into your briefcase and never blow a gasket again.

And hey, you might as well add "firefighter" to your business card.

This book has been bound
using handcraft methods and
Smyth-sewn to ensure durability.

Written by Sarah Royal.

Designed by Rachel Peckman.

Illustrated by Adam Howling.